W9-BVF-579

A BOUQUET OF
SUMMER
TASTES

CONTENTS

STARTERS

MAINS

SIDES

DESSERTS

Marinated Grilled Vegetables

These vegetables are wonderful served hot or cold, as a starter, part of the main course or in an antipasto platter with an assortment of cold meats, such as prosciutto and salami, and cheese, such as provolone and mozzarella. Artichoke hearts and black olives can also be added.

Makes 6 servings.

1	*large red onion*	1
2	*zucchini*	2
2	*small eggplants*	2
1	*red pepper*	1
1	*yellow pepper*	1
3	*Portobello mushrooms*	3
12	*button mushrooms*	12
1 tsp	*fresh thyme or ½ tsp (2 mL) dried*	5 mL
1 tsp	*fresh basil or ½ tsp (2 mL) dried*	5 mL
1 tsp	*fresh oregano or ½ tsp (2 mL) dried*	5 mL
¾ cup	*olive oil*	175 mL
¼ cup	*balsamic vinegar*	50 mL
3	*garlic cloves, minced*	3
½ tsp	*salt*	2 mL
½ tsp	*pepper*	2 mL

1. Cut all vegetables except mushrooms into ½-inch (12-mm) thick slices. Leave mushrooms whole.
2. To make marinade, whisk together herbs, oil, vinegar, garlic, salt and pepper. Arrange vegetables in a shallow dish, pour marinade over them, cover and refrigerate for 2 hours.
3. Prepare the barbecue. Grill the vegetables until they are tender, turning occasionally and brushing them with the marinade as they cook. Mushrooms and onions should take about 10 minutes, zucchini and eggplant about 15 minutes and peppers about 20 minutes.

Spicy Bloody Mary Soup

So good you might want to drink it instead of using a spoon.
Makes 6 servings.

1	medium onion, thinly sliced	1
3	celery stalks, finely diced	3
2 tbsp	olive oil	30 mL
3 tbsp	tomato purée	45 mL
6 cups	tomato juice or vegetable juice	1.5 L
2 tsp	Worcestershire sauce	10 mL
5 drops	Tabasco sauce	5 drops
1 tbsp	lemon juice	15 mL
½ cup	vodka	125 mL
	salt and lots of freshly ground pepper, to taste	
	celery leaves, for garnish	

1. Sauté onion and celery in olive oil until softened. Do not allow to brown.
2. Add tomato purée and mix thoroughly with vegetables. Cook for 1 minute. Add tomato juice and simmer for 10 minutes.
3. Add Worcestershire sauce, Tabasco, lemon juice, vodka and salt and pepper. Bring to boil and remove from heat.
4. Refrigerate and serve cold, garnished with celery leaves.

CORNING RECOMMENDS
REVERE® Stainless Steel Copper
Clad Bottom 8-qt Covered Stockpot
and CORELLE® IMPRESSIONS®
Fresh Cut Soup Bowls

Marinated Mushrooms with Herbs

Serve these as an appetizer and watch them disappear!
Makes 4–6 servings.

1 lb	mushrooms	500 g
½ cup	olive oil	125 mL
2 tbsp	lemon juice	30 mL
2 tbsp	white vinegar	30 mL
1 tsp	salt	5 mL
½ tsp	pepper	2 mL
1 tsp	dried tarragon, crumbled	5 mL
¼ tsp	dried thyme, crumbled	1 mL
¼ tsp	dried basil, crumbled	1 mL
1	garlic clove, minced	1

1. Clean mushrooms and put them into a saucepan.
2. Combine remaining ingredients and pour over mushrooms. Simmer over low heat for 8 minutes. Remove from heat and cool. Refrigerate in covered container overnight.
3. Serve at room temperature on their own, as an appetizer or as part of an antipasto platter.

CORNING RECOMMENDS
PYREX® Originals™ 1-cup
Measuring Cup and
PYREX® STORAGE PLUS®
7-cup Round Bowl with Cover

Pepper, Tomato and Tuna Antipasto

Everyone loves to mound this on crispy crackers or crostini as an appetizer.
Makes 4 servings.

2	red peppers	2
2	yellow peppers	2
3 tbsp	extra virgin olive oil	45 mL
3	garlic cloves, coarsely chopped	3
1 cup	chopped red onion	250 mL
4	plum tomatoes, seeded and cut into strips	4
¼ cup	coarsely chopped black olives	50 mL
3 tbsp	capers, drained and rinsed	45 mL
1	can (6 oz / 170 g) tuna, drained	1
2 tbsp	red wine vinegar	30 mL
	freshly ground black pepper	
¼ cup	chopped Italian parsley	50 mL

1. Roast peppers under broiler, turning as necessary, until skin is charred on all sides. Remove from oven and let stand until cool enough to handle. Remove skin and seeds. Cut pepper in half crosswise and then into strips. Place peppers in a shallow serving dish.
2. Heat 2 tbsp (30 mL) olive oil in small saucepan. Add garlic and onions and cook until softened but not brown. Spread onions over peppers.
3. Layer tomatoes, olives, capers and tuna over peppers. Whisk together remaining olive oil, vinegar and pepper. Pour over vegetables and tuna. Sprinkle with parsley.

Mango and Brie Quesadillas

This combination of mango and melted Brie is luscious, but you can try whatever combination of fruit and cheese that appeals to you — even good old apple and cheddar.

Makes 4 servings.

½ lb	Brie cheese, thinly sliced	250 g
6	small flour tortillas	6
I	large ripe mango, peeled and sliced	I

1. Divide half the slices of Brie evenly along the bottom half of each tortilla. Top with mango slices and the rest of the Brie slices. Fold in half.
2. Heat nonstick skillet over medium heat. Cook tortillas 2 to 3 minutes per side until cheese is melted and tortilla is browned.
3. To serve, cut in half.

CORNING RECOMMENDS

REVERE® Nonstick 12-inch Skillet and CORELLE® IMPRESSIONS® Oceanview Dinner Plate

Gazpacho

There is nothing better on a hot summer night than an icy cold bowl of gazpacho!
Makes 4 servings.

1	large cucumber, seeds removed	1
2	tomatoes	2
½	red pepper	½
½	green pepper	½
½	red onion	½
2	celery sticks	2
2	garlic cloves, minced	2
4 cups	tomato juice	1 L
4 tbsp	red wine vinegar	60 mL
½ tsp	salt	2 mL
	Tabasco to taste (optional)	

1. Finely dice cucumber, tomatoes, peppers, onion and celery. Place in bowl. Stir in the remaining ingredients. Refrigerate, covered, until very cold.
2. Serve with a good bread and Herb Butter.

Herb Butter

1 cup	butter, softened	250 mL
2	garlic cloves	2
2 tbsp	fresh basil	30 mL
2 tbsp	flat-leaf parsley	30 mL
1 tbsp	chives	15 mL
¼ cup	Parmesan cheese	50 mL

1. Combine all ingredients in a food processor until smooth.
2. Butter slices of bread and serve at room temperature or wrap in foil and warm in a 350°F (180°C) oven for 15 minutes.

CORNING RECOMMENDS
PYREX® Originals™ 1-qt
Measuring Cup and
CORNINGWARE® Casual
Elegance White Flora™ 2 ¼-qt
Round Dish with Covers

Summer Vegetable Medley

This is a great way to enjoy a variety of summer-fresh vegetables when they're in season.
Makes 4–6 servings.

2 tbsp	olive oil	30 mL
1	onion, quartered and thinly sliced	1
2	garlic cloves, thinly sliced	2
½ lb	baby carrots or larger carrots, sliced diagonally	250 g
½ lb	green or yellow beans, sliced diagonally or French cut	250 g
2	cobs corn, kernels removed	2
2	zucchini, cut in medium dice	2
1	red pepper, finely diced	1
¼ lb	snow peas, sugar snap peas or shelled peas	125 g
¼ cup	slivered fresh basil leaves	50 mL
1 tbsp	fresh oregano leaves	15 mL
1 tbsp	fresh thyme leaves	15 mL
	salt and pepper, to taste	

CORNING RECOMMENDS

REVERE® Stainless Aluminum Disc
Bottom 10-inch Covered Skillet,
CORELLE® IMPRESSIONS®
Oceanview 12 ¼" Serving Platter,
Soup Bowls, and PYREX®
STORAGE PLUS® Round Bowl

1. Heat oil in large skillet. Cook onion and garlic until just soft.
2. Add carrots and ½ cup (125 mL) water. Cover and cook over medium heat, about 4 minutes (depending on size of carrots), then add vegetables and cook about 6 to 8 minutes. If liquid evaporates, add more as necessary.
3. When all vegetables are just cooked through, remove cover and increase heat to cook off juices. Gently stir in herbs and season with salt and pepper.

Grilled Lemon Chicken

This is a perfect combination for an easy and light summer dish.
Makes 4 servings.

⅓ cup	*lemon juice*	75 mL
¼ cup	*olive oil*	50 mL
2	*garlic cloves, minced*	2
½ tsp	*salt*	2 mL
¼ tsp	*pepper*	1 mL
½ tsp	*dried thyme*	2 mL
4	*single, boneless, skinless chicken breasts*	4

1. Combine lemon juice, olive oil, garlic, salt, pepper and thyme in a small jar and shake well.
2. Put chicken in a shallow glass dish. Add marinade and cover tightly. Refrigerate overnight.
3. Remove chicken from marinade and grill on a preheated barbecue for 25 minutes. Serve with Mango Salsa.

CORNING RECOMMENDS
PYREX® STORAGE PLUS® 6-cup
Rectangular Dish with Cover and
CORELLE® IMPRESSIONS®
Enhancements Dinner Plate

Mango Salsa

2	*mangoes, peeled and diced*	2
¼ cup	*chopped red onion*	50 mL
¼ cup	*chopped red pepper*	50 mL
2	*garlic cloves, minced*	2
1 tbsp	*finely chopped parsley*	15 mL
2 tbsp	*lime juice*	30 mL
1 tbsp	*rice vinegar*	15 mL
pinch	*crushed red pepper flakes*	pinch

Combine all ingredients. Cover and refrigerate until serving.

Mediterranean Burgers

When you feel the urge for a juicy barbecued burger hot off the grill, don't look any further than this recipe.

Makes 4 servings.

1 lb	lean ground beef	500 g
2 tbsp	Dijon mustard	30 mL
2 tbsp	olive oil	30 mL
2 tbsp	dried oregano	30 mL
5	garlic cloves, pressed	5
	freshly ground black pepper, to taste	
	sliced tomatoes for topping	
	sliced mild or red onions for topping	

1. Mix together beef, mustard, oil, oregano, garlic and black pepper. Form into 4 burgers.
2. Preheat grill, and add burgers. Cook until meat is no longer pink in centre. Alternatively, broil in oven.
3. Serve in big, warmed crusty rolls with tomato and onion slices.

Simple Herbed Scallops

This recipe is so incredibly easy and so delicious. These scallops can be a main dish or served as a starter for an elegant dinner.

Makes 4 servings.

24	*large scallops*	24
2 tbsp	*butter, melted*	30 mL
2	*slices of brown bread*	2
1 tbsp	*Parmesan cheese*	15 mL
1 tbsp	*chopped fresh parsley*	15 mL
1 tbsp	*chopped fresh chives*	15 mL
	salt and pepper, to taste	
1	*lemon, cut into 4 wedges*	1

1. Preheat broiler. Rinse scallops and pat dry. Toss scallops with butter to coat well.

2. In a food processor, process bread, cheese, parsley, chives, salt and pepper until very fine. Dip one flat side of each scallop in the crumb mixture and place in a lightly buttered baking dish, crumb side up. Broil 5 minutes until scallops are opaque throughout. Serve with lemon wedges.

Scallops in Garlic Butter

½ cup	*butter*	125 mL
3	*garlic cloves, minced*	3
24	*large sea scallops*	24
	salt and pepper, to taste	
3 tbsp	*chopped parsley*	45 mL
1	*lemon, cut into thin wedges*	1

1. Melt butter over medium heat in a skillet. Add garlic and cook for 1 minute. Add scallops and salt and pepper and sauté for 5 minutes until opaque.

2. Serve over rice. Garnish with parsley and lemon wedges.

Pasta Niçoise

On a hot summer's night, this will make a perfect meal with some crusty bread and maybe a glass of chilled white wine!

Makes 4 servings.

I lb	pasta (penne, coloured corkscrews or bows)	500 g
¼ cup	lemon juice	50 mL
¼ cup	extra virgin olive oil	50 mL
¼ cup	diced red onion	50 mL
I	garlic clove, minced	I
¼ tsp	dried rosemary	I mL
	salt and pepper, to taste	
½ lb	green beans, halved lengthwise	250 g
I ½ cups	diced cooked (or barbecued) chicken	375 mL
3	plum tomatoes, cut into sixths	3
2	hard-boiled eggs, cut into eighths	2
¼ cup	chopped flat-leaf parsley	50 mL
I tbsp	capers, drained	I5 mL
	anchovy fillets and black olives, to taste	

1. Cook pasta in boiling salted water until just tender. Drain well and rinse with cold water. Shake off excess moisture.
2. Combine lemon juice, oil, onion, garlic, rosemary, salt and pepper. Pour half of dressing over pasta and toss well.
3. Cook beans until just tender. Drain, rinse with cold water and drain again. Toss beans with half of remaining dressing.
4. Arrange pasta in serving bowl. Surround with beans, chicken, tomatoes and eggs. Sprinkle remaining dressing over salad. Top with parsley, capers, anchovies and olives.

CORNING RECOMMENDS
PYREX® Originals™ I-pt
Measuring Cup and
CORELLE IMPRESSIONS®
Oceanview I-qt Serving Bowl
and Soup Bowl

Ranch Wraps

This is a tasty, quick and satisfying dinner dish that even the kids will devour.
Makes 4 servings.

¼ cup + 3 tbsp	olive oil	50 mL + 45 ml
2 tbsp	red wine vinegar	30 mL
2 tbsp	barbecue sauce	30 mL
1 tsp	Worcestershire sauce	5 mL
4	garlic cloves, minced	4
2 tsp	dry mustard	10 mL
1 tsp	salt	5 mL
¼ tsp	freshly ground black pepper	1 mL
¼ tsp	Tabasco sauce	1 mL
1 lb	lean sirloin beef strips	500 g
4	large flour tortillas	4
2	large yellow onions, sliced thickly	2
1	red pepper, in strips	1
2	tomatoes, finely diced	2
	sliced banana peppers, for garnish (optional)	
	sour cream, for garnish (optional)	

1. To make marinade, combine ¼ cup oil, vinegar, barbecue sauce, Worcestershire, 2 garlic cloves, mustard, salt, pepper and Tabasco. Add beef and stir to coat meat with marinade. Refrigerate at least 12 hours or overnight.

2. Heat 2 tbsp (30 mL) olive oil in a skillet, add onions, red pepper and 2 garlic cloves and cook until softened. Remove to a bowl.

3. Heat remaining 1 tbsp olive oil in skillet, remove beef strips from marinade and stir fry until browned. Add onions and pepper to pan. Cook 4 minutes.

4. Put tortillas on a glass pie plate and microwave for 20 seconds or wrap in foil and warm in a 350°F (180°C) oven for 15 minutes.

5. To serve, place tortilla on plate, mound with beef and onion mix, top with tomatoes, banana peppers and sour cream (if using) and roll up, or roll tortilla to fit inside drinking glass and fill with beef mix and garnishes.

Oriental Salmon

So easy, so fast, so good!

Makes 4 servings.

2 tbsp	*teriyaki sauce*	30 mL
4 tsp	*ginger root, peeled and grated*	20 mL
1 tsp	*sesame oil*	5 mL
2	*garlic cloves, minced*	2
4	*salmon steaks*	4
2	*limes*	2

1. Mix together teriyaki sauce, ginger, sesame oil and garlic in a small glass bowl. Brush mixture over both sides of the salmon steak.
2. Preheat barbecue to medium high. Place steaks on the grill and cook for 5 minutes on each side, or until the fish flakes easily with a fork. Serve with a squeeze of fresh lime.
3. Alternatively, grill on top of stove in a grill pan for 3 minutes per side, or until the fish flakes easily with a fork.

CORNING RECOMMENDS
PYREX® Originals™
8-oz Utility Dish and
CORELLE® IMPRESSIONS®
Oceanview Dinner Plate

Barbecued Saucy Ribs

Try these ribs hot off the grill with some cornbread and coleslaw!
Makes 6 servings.

2 cups	*puréed canned tomatoes*	500 mL
1 bottle	*beer*	1 bottle
½ cup	*brown sugar*	125 mL
¼ cup	*red wine vinegar or cider vinegar*	50 mL
¼ cup	*molasses*	50 mL
2 tbsp	*Dijon mustard*	30 mL
2 tbsp	*Worcestershire sauce*	30 mL
1 tsp	*dried oregano*	5 mL
1 tsp	*cumin*	5 mL
½ tsp	*dried thyme*	2 mL
½ tsp	*hot pepper sauce (or more, to taste)*	2 mL
½ tsp	*salt*	2 mL
4 lbs	*spareribs*	2 kg
1 tsp	*thyme*	5 mL

1. Combine all ingredients except spareribs and thyme in a large saucepan. Bring to a boil, reduce heat and cook sauce at medium-low for 30 to 40 minutes or until thick. Stir occasionally, especially when sauce starts to thicken.

2. Cut ribs into serving pieces. Place in a large saucepan along with thyme. Cover with cold water. Bring to a boil. Reduce heat and cook, covered, for 45 minutes, or until ribs are tender. Drain.

3. Place ribs in a large flat dish. Pour half the sauce over ribs, reserving half for later use. Rub sauce into ribs. Marinate from 30 minutes to overnight, refrigerated.

4. To cook, remove ribs from sauce. Brush barbecue grill with oil. Cook ribs over medium-high heat until heated through and browned, about 15 minutes. Brush with sauce and turn several times during cooking. Alternatively, bake in a 375°F (190°C) oven for 30 minutes, brushing with sauce and turning during baking.

Vegetable Paella with Saffron

Saffron is such a luxury because of its expense that you only want to use it when it's really worthwhile. This dish makes the grade.

Makes 4–6 servings.

3 tbsp	olive oil	45 mL
1	medium onion, diced	1
3	garlic cloves, minced	3
	hot pepper flakes to taste	
1 ½ cups	converted rice	375 mL
1	red pepper, diced	1
1	yellow pepper, diced	1
2	small plum tomatoes, diced	2
⅓ cup	dried mushrooms, soaked in hot water for 30 minutes, then drained	75 mL
¾ tsp	whole saffron, crushed	4 mL
½ tsp	herbes de Provence, or mix of rosemary, thyme and oregano	2 mL
3 cups	chicken stock, canned or homemade	725 mL
1 cup	thawed frozen peas	250 mL
	salt and pepper, to taste	

1. Heat oil in large saucepan. Add onion, garlic and pepper flakes. Cook until softened.
2. Add rice, stir well and cook 3 minutes. Stir in peppers, tomatoes, mushrooms, saffron, herbs and chicken stock.
3. Bring to a boil. Cover and cook over medium-low heat for 20 minutes.
4. Remove lid. Stir in peas. Season with salt and pepper. Let stand 5 minutes to heat peas. Serve.

Salmon Salad with Potatoes and Asparagus

When new potatoes and asparagus are in season, try this dish for its lovely combination of fresh flavours.

Makes 4 servings.

1 lb	salmon fillet, in one piece	500 g
1 lb	new potatoes, cut into chunks	500 g
1 lb	asparagus	500 g
¾ cup	olive oil	175 mL
¼ cup	red wine vinegar	75 mL
1 tbsp	lemon juice	15 mL
1 tsp	Dijon mustard	2 mL
1	garlic clove, minced	1
2 tbsp	capers	30 mL
	salt and pepper, to taste	
2 tbsp	shredded fresh basil	30 mL
4 cups	salad greens	1 L

1. Heat oven to 400°F (200°C). Put salmon in a roasting dish and cook 10 minutes, or until fish flakes easily with a fork. Remove and cool, then cut in 4 pieces.
2. Meanwhile, cook potatoes in boiling, salted water until tender. Drain. Cook asparagus until tender-crisp. Drain.
3. To make dressing, combine oil, vinegar, lemon juice, mustard, garlic, capers, salt and pepper and basil. Toss potatoes with a little of the dressing.
4. Toss salad greens with the remaining dressing and divide evenly onto 4 plates. Top each with ¼ of the potatoes, ¼ of the asparagus and a piece of salmon. Drizzle any remaining dressing over each piece of fish and the asparagus. Sprinkle extra basil over all before serving.

Grilled Lime Shrimp

This is excellent on its own — with a rice or pasta salad on the side — or superb on a Caesar salad.

Makes 4 servings.

4	*limes*	4
4 tbsp	*olive oil*	60 mL
4	*garlic cloves, pressed or finely minced*	4
1 lb	*large or jumbo shrimp, deveined and shelled*	500 g

1. Pierce limes with a fork; microwave on high for 30 seconds. Squeeze juice and place in glass bowl.
2. Add oil, garlic and shrimp. Marinate for 20 minutes.
3. Heat grill or preheat broiler. Thread shrimps on skewers and cook for about 1 minute per side. Do not overcook. Serve.

CORNING RECOMMENDS
BAKE 'N' STORE™
8-inch Square Baking Dish with Storage Cover and CORELLE® IMPRESSIONS® Enhancements Dinner Plate

Danforth Avenue Pork Souvlaki

Danforth Avenue in Toronto is home to the city's large Greek population. The restaurants in the area draw people from far and wide to savour their specialties, including everybody's favourite . . . souvlaki.

Makes 4 servings.

I lb	*boneless pork*	500 g
4 tbsp	*olive oil*	60 mL
4 tbsp	*lemon juice, freshly squeezed*	60 mL
3	*garlic cloves (or more, to taste), pressed*	3
I tsp	*dried oregano*	5 mL
	tzatziki, for garnish, homemade or store bought (optional)	

1. Cut pork into cubes about I-inch (2.5-cm) square, discarding any fat.
2. To make marinade, in a 2-qt (2-L) baking dish, mix olive oil, lemon, garlic and oregano. Add pork pieces to marinade and toss to coat. Cover with plastic wrap and refrigerate for at least 2 hours.
3. Remove pork pieces from marinade and discard marinade. Thread pork onto skewers. Either grill or broil kabobs until meat is no longer pink in the middle, roughly 4 minutes each side over medium heat.
4. Serve with tzatziki on the side.

Chicken Works Too!

Substitute boneless, skinless chicken breasts for the pork. You can leave the breasts whole or cut them into cubes or strips.

Lamb Souvlaki

Substitute boneless lamb pieces for the pork. Thread onto skewers and cook as directed.

Mild Chicken Curry with Fresh Ginger and Chutney

A delightful way to give chicken some zip.

Makes 4 servings.

3 tbsp	*olive oil*	45 mL
1	*large onion, coarsely chopped*	1
3	*garlic cloves, minced*	3
1 tbsp	*peeled and grated fresh ginger*	15 mL
2 tbsp	*curry powder*	30 mL
2 tbsp	*flour*	30 mL
3 cups	*chicken broth (homemade or canned and diluted)*	750 mL
½ tsp	*ground coriander (optional)*	2 mL
¼ cup	*freshly squeezed lemon juice*	50 mL
4–5	*single, boneless, skinless chicken breasts, cut into 1-inch (2.5-cm) chunks*	4–5
1 tbsp	*chutney*	15 mL
	Optional condiments: additional chutney, diced green peppers, chopped fresh tomato, minced green onion, diced fresh pineapple	

1. Heat oil in large skillet. Add onion and cook until translucent. Add garlic and ginger and cook for 1 minute.
2. Sprinkle curry over onion, garlic and ginger and stir into oil. Add flour and stir.
3. Add 1 cup (250 mL) broth very slowly while mixing into the flour to make a smooth paste. Add remaining broth, coriander, lemon juice and chicken pieces. Bring to a boil, cover and reduce heat. Simmer for 30 minutes.
4. If sauce isn't thick enough, remove cover from skillet and simmer until desired consistency is reached.
5. Stir in chutney and serve over rice with choice of condiments on the side.

Pizza Quesadillas for Kids

This is perfect to make when all the kids come over to watch a movie. It can be as simple as pepperoni pizza or "fully dressed."
Makes 6–8 servings.

2 cups	*pizza sauce or spaghetti sauce*	500 mL
8	*large flour tortillas*	8
3 cups	*grated cheese (mozzarella, cheddar or a combination)*	750 mL
½ lb	*sliced pepperoni*	250 g
½ tsp	*dried oregano*	2 mL
	Options: cubed ham, sliced onions, sliced mushrooms, tomatoes, olives or peppers	

1. Spread sauce over one side of all 8 tortillas. Sprinkle 4 tortillas with cheese. Then sprinkle pepperoni, oregano and any of the optional ingredients (in small amounts or quesadillas will fall apart in cooking) on the other 4 tortillas.
2. Flip tortilla with cheese upside down over pepperoni tortilla to form a sandwich.
3. Put nonstick skillet on medium heat. Cook each tortilla 2 to 3 minutes per side, or until cheese has melted and tortilla has browned.
4. Cut into quarters and serve.

Sam's Secret Spuds

If you've ever savoured those delicious soft baked potatoes in a Greek restaurant you know how good they are. Put this on your must-try list for tonight.
Makes 4 servings.

4	*large potatoes, peeled and cut into cubes*	4
2	*carrots, chopped*	2
3	*ribs of celery, chopped*	3
1	*onion, chopped*	1
2 cups	*chicken stock, homemade or canned*	500 mL
3 tbsp	*olive oil*	45 mL

1. Preheat oven to 350°F (180°C).
2. Put potatoes, carrots, celery and onion in a casserole dish. Cover with chicken stock and olive oil and bake for about 1 hour, stirring occasionally. Potatoes are done when they are fork-tender and most of the liquid has evaporated.

CORNING RECOMMENDS
CORNINGWARE® Little Dishes
15oz FRENCH WHITE® Oval
Casserole with lid

Shrimp and Tomato Salad

The jalapeño pepper gives this dish a nice spicy bite, but if it's not to your liking, leave it out. These shrimp are so flavourful hot off the barbecue you might want to double the recipe!

Makes 4 servings.

1 lb	shrimp, peeled and deveined	500 g
2 tbsp	tomato paste	30 mL
2 tbsp	coarse grain mustard	30 mL
¼ cup	green onions, chopped	50 mL
1 tbsp	finely chopped jalapeño pepper	15 mL
4 tbsp	lemon juice	60 mL
4 tbsp	olive oil	60 mL
4	medium tomatoes, diced	4
2 tbsp	chopped sun-dried tomato	30 mL
¼ cup	chopped parsley	50 mL

1. In a mixing bowl, combine shrimp with tomato paste, mustard, green onions, jalapeño pepper, 2 tbsp (30 mL) lemon juice and 2 tbsp (30 mL) olive oil.
2. Grill or broil shrimp until just done, 1 or 2 minutes per side (or bake between sheets of parchment paper at 425°F/225°C for 6 to 8 minutes). Cool.
3. In a mixing bowl, combine tomatoes, sun-dried tomato, 2 tbsp (30 mL) lemon juice, 2 tbsp (30 mL) olive oil and parsley. Toss with shrimp. Serve with crusty bread or on a bed of salad greens on a serving platter from which guests serve themselves.

Greek Pasta Salad

What a riot of flavours! This dish is so tasty that all you need on the side is something fairly plain like a simple piece of grilled chicken or warm crusty bread. **Makes 4 servings.**

1 lb	fusilli pasta	500 g
½	red pepper, chopped	½
½	green pepper, chopped	½
⅓	English cucumber, chopped	⅓
2	tomatoes, chopped	2
½ cup	red onion, chopped	125 mL
½ cup	feta cheese, crumbled	125 mL
½ cup	Kalamata olives	125 mL
¼ cup	chopped flat-leaf parsley	50 mL

Dressing

⅓ cup	olive oil	75 mL
2 tbsp	lemon juice	30 mL
2 tbsp	red wine vinegar	30 mL
1 tsp	dried oregano	5 mL
2	garlic cloves, minced	2
¼ tsp	salt	1 mL
	generous grinding of black pepper	

1. Cook pasta according to package directions. Drain and rinse in cold water. Refrigerate while chopping vegetables.
2. Chop vegetables. Combine all dressing ingredients in a jar and shake to blend.
3. Put cold pasta, cheese, olives and vegetables into a bowl and toss with dressing.

Greek Salad

Substitute 1 small Romaine lettuce, washed and torn into small pieces, for the pasta.

Deli-style Coleslaw

Perfect for a picnic or to enjoy on a hot summer day!
Makes 8 servings.

I	medium cabbage, shredded	I
I	carrot, shredded	I
½	medium red onion, finely minced	½
⅓ cup	sugar	75 mL
½ cup	white vinegar	I25 mL
¼ cup	vegetable oil	50 mL
2	garlic cloves, minced	2
½ tsp	salt	2 mL
	pepper, to taste	
½ tsp	caraway seeds (optional)	2 mL

1. Mix together cabbage, carrot and onion in a large glass or plastic bowl.
2. To make dressing, in a I-qt (I-L) saucepan, bring sugar, vinegar, oil, garlic, salt and pepper and caraway, if using, to a boil.
3. Quickly pour boiling dressing over cabbage mixture and toss thoroughly.
4. Refrigerate for at least 2 hours, mixing occasionally. Serve.

Deli-style Sub Sandwich

4	Kaiser-style rolls, or rolls of your choosing	4
I lb	thinly sliced cooked roast beef	500 g
	Dijon mustard	
	Deli-style Coleslaw	

Split rolls, spread with mustard, and mound on beef and a generous serving of coleslaw. Slice and serve.

Colourful Zesty Bean Salad

This is a tasty new version of the popular old standby. Take it along on a picnic or pack for a healthy lunch!

Makes 8 servings.

1	can (19 oz/540 mL) black beans	1
1	can (19 oz/540 mL) red kidney beans	1
1	can (19 oz/540 mL) chick peas	1
1	can (12 oz/341 mL) corn niblets	1
1 cup	celery, chopped	250 mL
½ cup	chopped red onion	125 mL
¼ cup	chopped parsley	50 mL
½ cup	vegetable oil	125 mL
¾ cup	sugar	175 mL
¾ cup	red wine vinegar	175 mL
1 tsp	salt	5 mL
½ tsp	pepper	2 mL

1. Put black beans, kidney beans, chick peas, corn, celery, onion and parsley into a 2 ½-qt (2.5-L) bowl.
2. Mix oil, sugar, vinegar, salt and pepper until blended. Pour over salad and toss.
3. Refrigerate for several hours or overnight.
4. To serve, drain off dressing and put into a bowl.

Ruby Fruit

With fresh fruits in season, now is the time to make this dessert and enjoy every bite!
Makes 8 servings.

1 cup	blueberries	250 mL
1 cup	raspberries	250 mL
1 cup	black raspberries	250 mL
1 cup	black currants (if available)	250 mL
2 cups	strawberries, hulled and quartered	500 mL
½ cup	strawberry jam	125 mL
¼ cup	black currant nectar (such as Ribena)	50 mL
2 tbsp	raspberry or other fruit liqueur (optional)	30 mL
	mint leaves, for garnish	

1. Combine fruit in a serving bowl.
2. Combine jam, nectar and liqueur in food processor or blender. Pour over fruit and let stand 1 hour before serving. Garnish with mint leaves. Serve with angel cake, ice cream, fruit sherbet or cookies.

Strawberry Delight

You haven't lived until you've treated yourself to this taste sensation!

Makes 4 servings.

1 quart	*fresh strawberries*	1 L
2 cups	*sour cream*	500 mL
2 cups	*brown sugar*	500 mL

1. Wash strawberries and dry on paper towels. Place berries in a bowl. Put sour cream in a smaller bowl and the brown sugar in another.
2. Each person takes a berry, dips it in the sour cream, then in the brown sugar.

S t r a w b e r r y   C a k e

Makes 6–8 servings.

1	*white cake mix*	1
1 cup	*whipping cream*	250 mL
2 tbsp	*sugar*	30 mL
½ tsp	*almond extract*	2 mL
4 cups	*strawberries, sliced*	1 L
	mint, for garnish	

Put One Away

Wrap second cake and put it in the freezer for future use.

1. Make cake according to directions on the package, using two 8-inch (20-cm) square cake dishes. Cool and remove both cakes from dishes.
2. Whip the cream, sugar and almond extract until soft peaks form. Cut one cake into serving-size pieces. Cut each piece in half. Put the bottom half on a serving plate. Top with whipped cream, strawberries, top half of the cake and more whipped cream and strawberries.
3. Serve with a sprig of mint for garnish.

Summer Fruit Trifle

Trifle is always a popular dessert; it's easy to make and has a delicious, creamy combination of flavours.

Makes 4–6 servings.

1	*frozen pound cake*	1
1	*package (10oz/284mL) frozen raspberries*	1
2 ½ cups	*vanilla custard* *(prepared from a custard powder mix or homemade)*	625 mL
1 cup	*whipping cream*	250 mL
3 tbsp	*rum or Amaretto (optional)*	45 mL
1 cup	*blueberries*	250 mL
2 cups	*sliced strawberries*	500 mL
	whole strawberries and sliced kiwi, for garnish	

1. Thaw pound cake and raspberries.
2. Make a batch of vanilla custard following package instructions or recipe. Set aside to cool. Whip the cream.
3. Slice the pound cake into ¼-inch (6-mm) slices. Cover the bottom of a 10-cup (2.5-L) bowl with the cake slices, then put one layer of cake slices around the sides of the bowl. Put any remaining cake on the bottom. Sprinkle with rum, if using.
4. Spread the thawed raspberries on top of the cake, then add the blueberries in a layer. Cover with the cooled custard. Arrange the sliced strawberries on top of the custard and top with the whipped cream.
5. Garnish with whole strawberries and kiwi slices.

CORNING RECOMMENDS
PYREX® STORAGE PLUS®
7-cup Round Bowls with
Dark Teal Plastic Cover

Luscious Warm Summer Fruit with Cream

The name of this recipe says it all!

Makes 6 servings.

8	*ripe peaches, peeled and sliced*	8
1 cup	*blueberries*	250 mL
1 tsp	*cinnamon*	5 mL
1 tbsp	*lemon juice*	15 mL
1 cup	*cream, whipped to form stiff peaks*	250 mL
½ cup	*brown sugar*	125 mL

1. Layer peaches in 2-qt (2-L) shallow baking dish. Scatter blueberries over top and sprinkle with cinnamon and lemon juice.
2. Spread cream over fruit and sift sugar evenly over cream.
3. Cover with plastic wrap and refrigerate for at least 12 hours.
4. Before serving, preheat broiler; broil fruit for about 2 minutes, or until golden.

Homemade Ice Cream Sandwich Cookies

Kids love to buy these at the local convenience store — where they're very expensive. You can make these together at home and be as creative as you like. **Makes 8 servings.**

1 qt	ice cream (vanilla, chocolate chip, chocolate or your favourite flavour)	1 L
16	large oatmeal cookies (the very hard and crunchy type)	16
1 cup	miniature chocolate chips, chocolate or coloured sprinkles or candy (such as mini M&Ms) (optional)	250 mL
½ cup	regular chocolate chips	125 mL

Put One Away

Double the recipe and after cookies have frozen completely, store them in an airtight freezer bag.

CORNING RECOMMENDS

PYREX® Originals™ 1-cup Measuring Cup and PYREX® Originals™ 9 ½" Flavor Saver™ Pie Plate

1. Remove ice cream from freezer and allow to soften for 30 minutes or to spreading consistency.
2. Spread 8 oatmeal cookies in a single layer on a cookie sheet or baking pan.
3. Heap some ice cream onto the centre of each cookie. (Don't worry about it reaching the edge of the cookie; when the top cookie is put on, the ice cream will be pressed to the edge.) Put a cookie on top of each and press to flatten slightly.
4. Put miniature chocolate chips, sprinkles or candy in a pie plate. Press the sides of each cookie sandwich into the pie plate to coat the edge with the chips, sprinkles or candy. Put the sandwiches in the freezer to keep cold.
5. As an option, in the microwave, melt chocolate chips in a glass measuring cup. Remove sandwiches from freezer and, using a spoon, drizzle melted chocolate on top of each cookie. Freeze the sandwiches.

Raspberry Cheesecake

This is a wonderful dessert to serve guests — can you ever have enough raspberries?
Makes 10–12 servings.

1 ½ cups	*graham wafer crumbs*	375 mL
4 tbsp	*melted butter*	60 mL
2 tbsp	*sugar*	30 mL
3	*packages (8 oz / 750 g each) cream cheese*	3
1 cup	*sugar*	250 mL
3 tbsp	*flour*	45 mL
2 tbsp	*lemon juice*	30 mL
½ tsp	*vanilla*	2 mL
3	*eggs*	3
1	*package (10 oz / 284 mL) frozen raspberries*	1
1 tsp	*cold water*	5 mL
1 tsp	*cornstarch*	5 mL

1. Preheat oven to 325°F (160°C).
2. To make crust, combine crumbs, butter and sugar. Press mixture into bottom of a 9-inch (23-cm) springform pan. Bake for 10 minutes. Remove from oven. Increase heat to 425°F (225°C).
3. To make filling, in a large mixing bowl, beat cream cheese, sugar, flour, juice and vanilla until smooth. Add eggs, one at a time, beating well after each addition. Pour filling over crust.
4. Bake for 10 minutes. Reduce heat to 250°F (120°C) and bake for 30 to 35 minutes longer, or until centre of cake is barely firm. Remove from oven and run knife around the sides of the cake. Cool completely before removing sides. Chill until firm.
5. To make topping, thaw raspberries and bring them to a boil in a small saucepan. Add water to the cornstarch, then add to the berries. Cook for 30 seconds, stirring constantly until thickened. Cool and spread over cheesecake.

CORNING RECOMMENDS
PYREX® Originals™ 2-qt Oblong
Baking Dish, PYREX® Originals™
OVENWARE 4-qt Mixing Bowl
and CORELLE® IMPRESSIONS®
Fresh Cut Dessert/Salad Plate

Index

Produced exclusively for Corning Canada Inc., 60 Leek Crescent, Richmond Hill, Ontario Canada L4B 1H1 by Alpha Corporation/Susan Yates, Publisher

Photographs by Peter Paterson/Paterson Photographic Works Inc.

Copy Editor: Wendy Thomas

Editorial Services: Colborne Communications Centre

Text Cover and Design: Dave Murphy/Artplus Ltd.

Page Layout: Valerie Bateman & Leanne Knox/Artplus Ltd.

Printed and bound in Canada by Transcontinental Printing Inc.

For product information call: 905-771-3575

ISBN: 1-896391-23-0

Distributed by Canadian Tire Corporation